ONE POT

ONE POT

PERFECTLY PREPARED TO ENJOY EVERY DAY

This edition published in 2012

LOVE FOOD is an imprint of Parragon Books Ltd

Parragon
Queen Street House
4 Queen Street
Bath BA1 1HE, UK

Copyright © Parragon Books Ltd 2012

www.parragon.com

ISBN: 978-1-4454-6755-9

Printed in China

Concept: Patrik Jaros & Günter Beer
Recipes and food styling: Patrik Jaros www.foodlook.com
Text: Günter Beer, Gerhard von Richthofen, Patrik Jaros, Jörg Zipprick
Photography: Günter Beer www.beerfoto.com
Photographer's assistants: Sigurd Buchberger, Aranxa Alvarez
Cook's assistants: Magnus Thelen, Johannes von Bemberg
Designed by Estudio Merino www.estudiomerino.com
Produced by Buenavista Studio s.l. www.buenavistastudio.com
The visual index is a registered design of Buenavista Studio s.l. (European Trademark Office number 000252796-001)
Project management: trans texas publishing, Cologne
Typesetting: Nazire Ergün, Cologne

Notes for the Reader
This book uses both metric and imperial measurements. Follow the same units of measurement throughout; do not mix metric and imperial. All spoon measurements are level: teaspoons are assumed to be 5 ml, and tablespoons are assumed to be 15 ml. Unless otherwise stated, milk is assumed to be full fat, eggs and individual vegetables are medium, and pepper is freshly ground black pepper.

The times given are an approximate guide only. Preparation times differ according to the techniques used by different people and the cooking times may also vary from those given. Optional ingredients, variations or serving suggestions have not been included in the calculations.

Recipes using raw or very lightly cooked eggs should be avoided by infants, the elderly, pregnant women, convalescents and anyone suffering from an illness. Pregnant and breastfeeding women are advised to avoid eating peanuts and peanut products. Sufferers from nut allergies should be aware that some of the ready-made ingredients used in the recipes in this book may contain nuts. Always check the packaging before use.

Picture acknowledgements
All photos by Günter Beer, Barcelona

Contents

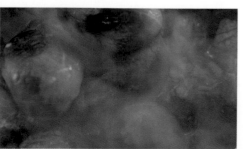

Introduction

If you don't fancy raiding your cupboards and battling with several pots and pans to produce one meal, this is just the right book for you. Although the delicious dishes here are cooked in saucepans, casseroles, woks, pie dishes or frying pans, the advantage of these recipes is that only one pot is ever needed! You don't have the hassle of matching saucepans with lids or working on limited hob rings – not to mention not having to worry about washing up piles of dirty pots after your meal.

Using just one pot has other advantages. It's easy, and it saves both energy and time because either the dish cooks quickly in a wok or frying pan, or it stews slowly in the oven in a casserole or pie dish, allowing you to get on with other things in the meantime. And something that should not be underestimated with one-pot dishes is their flavour. All the ingredients cook together in their own juices and develop their own unique and delicious aroma.

If you think only soups or stews can be cooked in one pot, you will be amazed at the diversity of our one-pot suggestions. The choice of recipes in this book includes vegetarian dishes as well as meat, fish and seafood recipes. We feature soups and stews, curries, ragouts and rice and

pasta dishes, including international specialties and culinary classics, some warm and hearty, some exotic and spicy.

The spectrum of countries whose culinary traditions we sample ranges from Hungary (goulash), Spain (paella), Italy (risotto), Ireland (Irish Stew) and USA (squash soup) to India (biryani) and Vietnam (beef with ginger). There are wholesome dishes, such as Tomato Bean Stew with Spicy Lamb Sausage and Sour Vegetable & Lentil Stew, alongside more refined cuisine for special occasions, such as Stuffed Pigeons Wrapped in Bacon, Lobster Bisque or Duck Breast with Orange-pepper Sauce.

Pots and pans

Every household is equipped with pots, pans and pie dishes. It's also useful to invest in a casserole, roaster and wok. The quality of the dishes is important. Pots and pans should be a reasonable weight and have a thick base that will conduct the heat well and prevent the contents burning. Make sure you choose the right size for your recipe. If the saucepan is too small, the contents will cook unevenly and cannot be stirred properly. In an oversized pot, the liquid will evaporate too quickly and the food is more likely to burn. The most frequently used pots and pans are the following:

Pie and gratin dishes: these heat-resistant dishes made of different kinds of materials are ideal for preparing bakes and other oven-cooked dishes. Some pie dishes can also be used on the hob.

Roasters: a large pan with a heavy lid for cooking meat. A roaster is ideal for preparing larger joints of meat or poultry that are cooked whole. They are usually big enough to cook vegetables in too. Roasting in the juices of the meat, they develop a wonderful flavour.

Casserole: a covered casserole is ideal for preparing dishes which simmer for a long time either in the oven or on the hob. Casseroles are available with two handles or a single handle. When covered, ingredients can develop their full flavours.

Paella pan: a large flat pan in which the classic Spanish dish is prepared. A conventional high-sided pan, however, can also be used.

Wok: a conical cooking pot with a rounded base. The wok gets hottest in the centre. Ingredients are cooked here or pushed aside as required. Woks are usually used to stir-fry vegetables and meat. They are available with two handles or a single handle on one side. If you have an electric hob, you'll need a flat-based wok.

Other cooking utensils

Wooden spoon: with a wooden spoon you can stir ingredients easily without damaging the base of your pot or pan. This is especially important if the pan has a non-stick or enamel coating.

Fish slice: a fish slice is particularly useful for stir-frying ingredients, for example in a wok.

Meat fork: larger joints of meat can be turned and, if required, removed from a pan with a meat fork.

Slotted spoon: a slotted spoon can be used to skim excess fat from the top of stews and casseroles.

Ingredients

There is virtually nothing that cannot be cooked in a single pot. However, a number of rules should be observed:

If the dish is prepared with meat or poultry, sear these briefly before adding the other ingredients. The meat cooks more quickly in this way and you will have a wonderfully aromatic gravy.

Do remember that different ingredients require different cooking times. Generally speaking, harder ingredients take longer to cook and should be added first, softer ingredients shoud be added later.

Leafy greens should only be cooked briefly so that they stay crisp and retain their bright colour. This will also prevent them overpowering the flavour of the other vegetables. Dried pulses should be soaked overnight and boiled for at least 10 minutes before being added to the pot.

Home-made stock, of course, tastes best. But if you're in a hurry or baulk at the effort involved in preparing your own, instant products are a good alternative. However, do make sure the stock is not too salty. There are numerous high-quality instant products available today, ranging from stock cubes to cartons of fresh stock.

Alcohol can enhance the flavour of many casserole and stews, but do make sure that it reaches boiling point and that you cook it off for a few minutes. The liquid will reduce, leaving a wonderfully rich gravy or sauce.

How to use this book

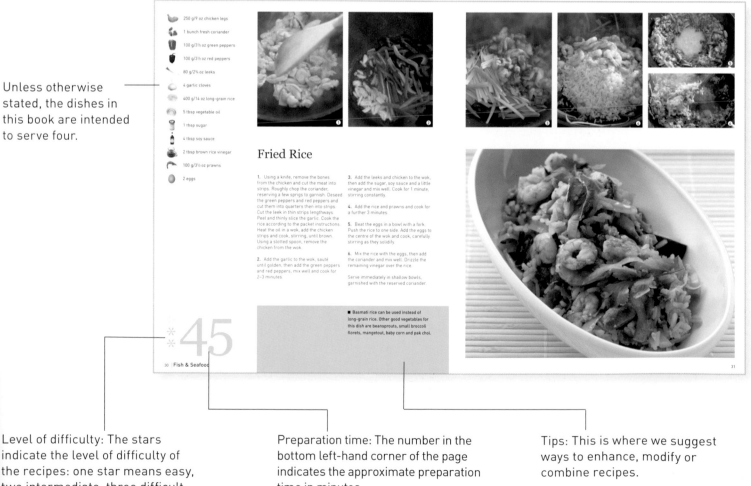

Unless otherwise stated, the dishes in this book are intended to serve four.

Fried Rice

1. Using a knife, remove the bones from the chicken and cut the meat into strips. Roughly chop the coriander, reserving a few sprigs to garnish. Deseed the green peppers and red peppers and cut them into quarters then into strips. Cut the leek in thin strips lengthways. Peel and thinly slice the garlic. Cook the rice according to the packet instructions. Heat the oil in a wok, add the chicken strips and cook, stirring, until brown. Using a slotted spoon, remove the chicken from the wok.

2. Add the garlic to the wok, sauté until golden, then add the green peppers and red peppers, mix well and cook for 2–3 minutes.

3. Add the leeks and chicken to the wok, then add the sugar, soy sauce and a little vinegar and mix well. Cook for 1 minute, stirring constantly.

4. Add the rice and prawns and cook for a further 3 minutes.

5. Beat the eggs in a bowl with a fork. Push the rice to one side. Add the eggs to the centre of the wok and cook, carefully stirring as they solidify.

6. Mix the rice with the eggs, then add the coriander and mix well. Drizzle the remaining vinegar over the rice.

Serve immediately in shallow bowls, garnished with the reserved coriander.

■ Basmati rice can be used instead of long-grain rice. Other good vegetables for this dish are beansprouts, small broccoli florets, mangetout, baby corn and pak choi.

Ingredients:
- 250 g/9 oz chicken legs
- 1 bunch fresh coriander
- 100 g/3½ oz green peppers
- 100 g/3½ oz red peppers
- 80 g/2¾ oz leeks
- 4 garlic cloves
- 400 g/14 oz long-grain rice
- 5 tbsp vegetable oil
- 1 tbsp sugar
- 4 tbsp soy sauce
- 2 tbsp brown rice vinegar
- 100 g/3½ oz prawns
- 2 eggs

45

30 | Fish & Seafood

31

Level of difficulty: The stars indicate the level of difficulty of the recipes: one star means easy, two intermediate, three difficult.

Preparation time: The number in the bottom left-hand corner of the page indicates the approximate preparation time in minutes.

Tips: This is where we suggest ways to enhance, modify or combine recipes.

4 tbsp olive oil

 2 tbsp sugar

 70 g/2½ oz celery, finely diced

 140 g/5 oz carrots, finely diced

 150 g/5½ oz onions, finely diced

 2 garlic cloves

 4 cloves

 2 lemon peel strips

 1 tsp white peppercorns, crushed

 1 fresh rosemary sprig

 1 fresh thyme sprig

 1 bay leaf

 1 tbsp tomato purée

 1.25 kg/2 lb 12 oz tomatoes, quartered

 1 tsp salt

 700 ml/1¼ pints chicken stock

Tomato Soup with Basil Croûtons

1. Pour the oil into a large saucepan. Add the sugar and gently sauté, then add the celery, carrots and onions. Gently sauté for 5 minutes. Peel the garlic cloves, cut in half and add to the pan with the cloves, lemon peel, peppercorns, rosemary, thyme and bay leaf. Sauté for a further 5 minutes.

2. Add the tomato purée and sauté for 1 minute, then add the tomatoes and salt.

3. Pour in the stock and bring to the boil over a high heat. Reduce the heat to medium and simmer for 20 minutes.

4. Remove what is left of the herb sprigs and the bay leaf and purée the ingredients in the pan for 1 minute using a hand-held blender.

5. Using a ladle, pour the soup through a fine sieve, pushing it through until the remnants are almost dry. This binds the soup and enhances the flavour.

Transfer the soup to warmed bowls and serve with basil croûtons.

■ For the basil croûtons, melt 20 g/¾ oz butter in a non-stick frying pan, add 50 g/1¾ oz cubed white bread and fry, stirring constantly, until golden brown. Add 4 basil leaves, cut into ribbons, season with salt and mix together. Remove the croûtons from the heat to prevent them burning and set aside in a bowl until needed.

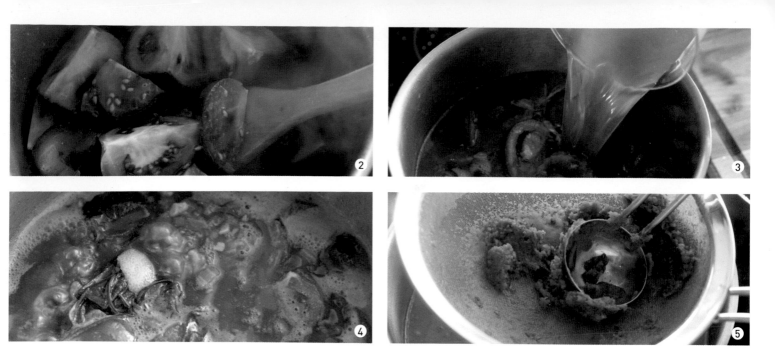

1.6 kg/3 lb 8 oz squash

 ½ bunch fresh dill

 15 g/½ oz fresh ginger

 1 garlic clove

 80 g/2¾ oz carrots

 150 g/5½ oz red peppers

 30 g/1 oz celery

 80 g/2¾ oz onions

 40 g/1½ oz butter

 salt

 freshly grated nutmeg

 3 cloves

 1 bay leaf

 1 tsp tomato ketchup

 ½ tsp curry powder

 1½ tsp sweet paprika

 1 litre/1¾ pints chicken stock

 200 ml/7 fl oz cream

 100 ml/3½ fl oz crème fraîche

American-style Squash Soup with Cheese Croûtons

1. Cut the top off the squash from about 3 cm/1¼ inches down. Scrape out the seeds with a soup spoon. Finely chop the dill.

2. Using a melon baller, scoop out the flesh from the squash and the top, without damaging the skin. Leave about a 1-cm/½-inch thick wall. Reserve the flesh.

3. Peel the ginger and garlic and thinly slice. Cut the carrots, red peppers, celery and onions into 1-cm/½-inch pieces. Melt the butter in a large saucepan, add the garlic and onions and cook over a low heat until translucent. Add the carrots, red peppers, celery and ginger and cook for a further 5 minutes.

4. Add the squash flesh. Season to taste with salt and nutmeg, then add the cloves and bay leaf. Cook over a medium heat for about 10 minutes, until the squash begins to fall apart easily. Push it to one side.

5. Add the tomato ketchup, curry powder and paprika to the centre of the pan and cook for 1 minute, then mix in the squash.

6. Pour in the stock, bring to the boil and simmer over a medium heat for 15 minutes. Add the cream and crème fraîche and bring back to the boil.

 ✳ ✳ ✳ 60

■ Cheese croûtons: Cut half a baguette into 5-mm/¼-inch thick slices, sprinkle with 60 g/2¼ oz grated aged Gouda cheese and bake in the oven at 200°C/400°F/Gas Mark 6 for 5 minutes.

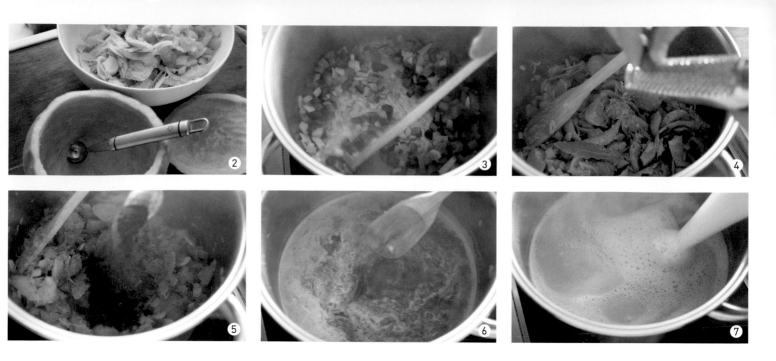

7. Purée with a hand-held blender for 1 minute, then pass it through a fine sieve. Use a ladle to press the liquid out of the remnants.

Pour the soup into the hollowed-out squash, sprinkle with the dill and serve with the cheese croûtons.

500 g/1 lb 2 oz dried chickpeas

 220 g/8 oz onions

 200 g/7 oz aubergines

 3 garlic cloves

 200 g/7 oz tomatoes

 5 tbsp sunflower oil

 1 tbsp star anise seeds

 6 cardamom pods

 8 cloves

 1 cinnamon stick

 salt and pepper

 1 tsp ground coriander

 1 tsp ground turmeric

 1.5 litres/2¾ pints water or vegetable stock

 200 g/7 oz natural yogurt

 pinch of ground cinnamon

 few drops of lemon juice

 2 fresh mint sprigs, shredded

Indian Chickpea Curry with Cinnamon Yogurt & Mint

1. Soak the chickpeas in cold water for at least 2 hours. Finely dice the onions. Cut the aubergine into 2-cm/¾-inch pieces. Peel the garlic and thinly slice. Peel the tomatoes and cut them into quarters. Heat the oil in a large saucepan over a medium heat, add the garlic and cook until golden brown. Add the anise seeds, cardamom pods, cloves and cinnamon stick and sauté.

2. Add the onions, cook until translucent, then push to the side of the pan. Add the aubergine to the centre of the pan, season to taste with salt and pepper and fry for 5 minutes.

3. Sprinkle with the coriander and turmeric and cook for 5 minutes until the onions and aubergine are slightly mushy. Drain the soaked chickpeas.

4. Add the chickpeas to the pan and cook briefly, then add the tomatoes and water.

5. Cover with a lid and simmer over a medium heat for 70 minutes. The chickpeas should remain submerged. Mix the yogurt with the ground cinnamon, lemon juice and mint.

Serve in bowls with the yogurt mix on the side.

+ 2 hours' soaking

※
※**100**
※

■ If possible, soak the chickpeas overnight. They will soften faster while cooking. This dish can also be served with roast beef or fried eggs.

1 carrot

 2 celery sticks

 1 leek

 1 onion

 2 tbsp oil

 1 tbsp butter

 1 tbsp tomato purée

 250 g/9 oz red lentils, rinsed and drained

 150 ml/5 fl oz white wine

 500 ml/18 fl oz stock

 salt and pepper

 ½ tsp dried marjoram

 2 tbsp vinegar

 2 tsp Dijon mustard

2 fresh parsley sprigs, chopped, to garnish

Sour Vegetable & Lentil Stew

1. Finely dice the carrot, celery and leek, reserving a few celery leaves to garnish. Dice the onion.

2. Heat the oil and butter in a large saucepan over a high heat, add the vegetables and sauté, then add the tomato purée and stir.

3. Add the lentils to the vegetables and sauté.

4. Add the wine and bring to the boil. Add the stock and simmer for about 20 minutes.

5. Add salt and pepper to taste and stir in the marjoram. Add the vinegar and mustard.

Garnish with chopped parsley and celery leaves and serve.

■ This is an outstanding side dish with grilled fish or roasted whole pigeon, or it can be served with a few crispy bacon rashers. The lentils can also be rounded off with finely chopped anchovies, capers, gherkins or even a little whipped cream.

½ tsp caraway seeds

 4½ tbsp vegetable oil

 500 g/1 lb 2 oz seitan

 1 garlic clove, chopped

 1 tsp chopped fresh marjoram

 salt and pepper

 3 onions

 500 g/1 lb 2 oz floury potatoes, peeled and cubed

 2 tbsp sweet paprika

 1 litre/1¾ pints vegetable stock

 1 tsp snipped fresh chives, to garnish

Vegetarian Goulash with Potatoes & Paprika

1. Drizzle the caraway seeds with some of the oil and finely chop. The oil helps the seeds to stay on the chopping board.

2. Cut the seitan into cubes and marinate for 10 minutes with the garlic, caraway seeds, marjoram, and salt and pepper to taste.

3. Heat the remaining oil in a large saucepan. Slice the onions into strips, add to the pan and sauté, then add the potatoes.

4. Dust with the paprika and stir well.

5. Add the marinated seitan to the potatoes and mix.

6. Add the stock and simmer for about 30 minutes.

Transfer to bowls, sprinkle with chives and serve.

■ Adding other vegetables such as red and yellow peppers, courgettes and pieces of tomato adds zest to the goulash and gives it a fresh and fruity flavour. Seitan is a tasty substitute for beef or pork. If you like goulash really hot, then replace half the sweet paprika with hot paprika.

30 g/1 oz bacon rashers

 250 g/9 oz tomatoes

 1 garlic clove

 1 shallot

 6 artichokes

 80 g/2¾ oz butter

 4 tbsp olive oil

 pinch of sugar

 salt and pepper

 250 g/9 oz arborio rice

 750 ml/1¼ pints chicken stock

 2 fresh rosemary sprigs

 90 g/3¼ oz freshly grated Parmesan cheese

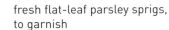 fresh flat-leaf parsley sprigs, to garnish

Tomato & Artichoke Risotto

1. Cut the bacon into 1-cm/½-inch wide strips. Peel the tomatoes and cut them into 1-cm/½-inch pieces. Finely chop the garlic and shallot. Cut the artichokes into sixths.

2. Heat 2 tablespoons of the butter and 2 tablespoons of the oil in a non-stick frying pan until foaming, then add the shallot and garlic and cook until translucent. Add the tomatoes, sugar, and salt and pepper to taste and simmer for about 2 minutes.

3. Add the rice and stir with a wooden spoon, then add the stock until the rice is just covered. The risotto should only be tossed from now on, not stirred. Simmer the risotto for about 15–18 minutes, adding the remaining hot stock gradually.

4. Meanwhile, heat the remaining oil in a separate non-stick frying pan, add the artichokes, rosemary, and salt and pepper to taste and gently sauté for about 5 minutes.

5. Add the bacon and fry until crisp. Remove the rosemary and add the artichokes and bacon to the risotto. Add the cheese and the remaining butter and stir.

Transfer to deep bowls and serve immediately, garnished with parsley.

■ Mushroom risotto: Clean 250 g/9 oz of mushrooms and cut into quarters or sixths. Heat 2 tablespoons of olive oil in a non-stick frying pan, add the mushrooms and sauté for 5 minutes until light brown. Add salt and pepper to taste. Peel ½ a garlic clove, finely chop and add to the mushrooms. Finely chop the leaves of ½ a bunch of parsley and add to the garlic and mushrooms. Drizzle over the juice of ½ a lemon and then tip into the risotto at the end of Step 2. Stir in 90 g/3¼ oz of freshly grated Parmesan cheese and serve immediately.

2 red peppers

 1 green pepper

 3 young onions

 500 g/1 lb 2 oz potatoes

 2 garlic cloves

 rind of 1 lemon

 ½ tsp caraway seeds

 3 tbsp vegetable oil

 2 tsp ground sweet paprika

 salt and pepper

 1.2 litres/2 pints vegetable stock

Vegetable Goulash

1. Halve and deseed the red and green peppers and cut them into 2-cm/¾-inch pieces. Roughly dice the onions. Peel the potatoes, cut into 2-cm/¾-inch pieces and set aside, covered with cold water. Peel the garlic cloves and finely chop with the lemon rind. Prepare the caraway seeds by drizzling some oil on them and then chopping them.

2. Heat the oil in a large saucepan, then add the onions and sauté. Drain the potato pieces in a colander. Add the potatoes to the pan and sauté gently for 5 minutes.

3. Sprinkle the garlic, lemon rind, caraway seeds and paprika over the potatoes and onions, and gently sweat.

4. Add the red peppers and green pepper, season to taste with salt and pepper, and cook for a few minutes over a medium heat.

5. Pour in the stock and simmer for about 25 minutes, stirring occasionally.

Ladle the goulash into deep bowls and serve with rye bread.

■ Courgettes and whole cherry tomatoes can be used instead of the peppers.

250 g/9 oz broccoli

 1 green pepper

 1 garlic clove

 250 g/9 oz rice noodles

 2 large green chillies

 5 tbsp vegetable oil

 2 tbsp Thai fish sauce

 2 tbsp soy sauce

 1 tbsp sugar

 2 eggs, beaten

 1 tbsp toasted sesame seeds, to garnish

Rice Noodles with Broccoli & Green Chillies

1. Cut off the broccoli florets. Halve, core and deseed the green pepper and thinly slice into 5-cm/2-inch strips. Finely chop the garlic.

2. Cook the rice noodles according to the packet instructions, then refresh them under cold running water and leave to drain. Slice the chillies into thin rings.

3. Heat a large wok over a high heat. Add 3 tablespoons of the oil, then add the broccoli and fry for about 5 minutes, stirring frequently. Add the fish sauce, then remove the broccoli and set aside.

4. Add the remaining oil to the wok, then add the garlic and fry. Add the noodles, then add the green pepper. Add the soy sauce and sprinkle over the sugar.

5. Return the broccoli to the wok and stir. Slowly add the eggs to the side of the wok and stir into the mixture. Add the chilli rings.

Transfer to deep bowls, sprinkle with sesame seeds and serve immediately.

■ Other fresh garnishes and herbs, such as chives, Thai basil, coriander or beansprouts, also complement this dish.

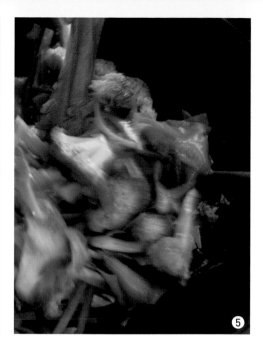

100 g/3½ oz onion

 3 shallots

 80 g/2¾ oz carrots

 80 g/2¾ oz celery

 3 garlic cloves

 10 black peppercorns

 1.2 kg/2 lb 12 oz lobster

 3 tbsp olive oil

 4 tbsp butter

 2 fresh thyme sprigs, roughly chopped

 1 fresh rosemary sprig, roughly chopped

 2 bay leaves, roughly chopped

 4 canned chopped plum tomatoes

 15 g/½ oz short-grain rice

 4 tbsp dry vermouth
4 tbsp cognac

 150 ml/5 fl oz white wine

 1 litre/1¾ pints shellfish stock

 400 ml/14 fl oz cream

 2 basil leaves

 salt

 cayenne pepper

①

Lobster Bisque

1. Cut the onions, shallots, carrots and celery into 5-mm/¼-inch pieces. Crush the garlic in its skin. Crush the peppercorns with a knife. Crack open the lobster and reserve the flesh. Heat the oil in a wide saucepan, then add the lobster shells and sauté for about 5 minutes. Add the butter and continue to sauté.

2. Add the chopped vegetables, garlic, peppercorns and chopped herbs, and cook until translucent. Scrape any residue from the base of the pan to prevent it burning.

3. Add the tomatoes and cook. Add the rice, vermouth, cognac and wine, bring to the boil and cook for a further 5 minutes until the alcohol evaporates.

4. Pour in the shellfish stock and simmer for 20 minutes.

5. Add the cream and basil and simmer for a further 1 minute. Carefully blend the soup with a hand-held blender on the lowest speed. Using a ladle, pass the soup through a fine sieve into a clean saucepan, squeezing out the shells. Bring back to the boil and season to taste with salt and cayenne pepper.

Serve the soup in deep bowls, placing 30 g/1 oz of the reserved lobster flesh in each bowl.

✳✳✳ 70

■ This soup takes its name from the salty, grated biscuits with which it was previously associated. Lobster bisque tastes even better if you start with the shells of live lobsters.

3 shallots

 60 g/2¼ oz celery

 1 leek

 1 garlic clove

 2 tbsp butter

 2 bay leaves

 1 fresh thyme sprig

 salt and pepper

 2 kg/4 lb 8 oz mussels, cleaned and debearded

 150 ml/5 fl oz white wine

 ½ bunch fresh parsley, finely chopped

Mussels Steamed in White Wine

1. Peel the shallots and cut them into fine strips. Slice the celery and leek into fine strips. Press the garlic clove in its skin. Melt the butter in a saucepan. Add the garlic and shallots, then add the bay leaves, thyme, celery and leek and sauté briefly. Season to taste with salt and pepper.

2. Add the mussels and mix with the vegetables. Pour in the wine, cover the pan and leave to simmer for 3–5 minutes until the mussels open. Sprinkle the parsley over the mussels.

Mix well and serve immediately.

✳
✳ 30
✳

■ Use an empty mussel shell to eat the cooked mussels without cutlery.

750 g/1 lb 10 oz fresh peas in their pods

 2 red peppers

 2 green peppers

 5 tbsp extra virgin olive oil

 1 kg/2 lb 4 oz short-grain rice

 200 ml/7 fl oz white wine

 salt and pepper

 pinch of ground saffron

 2 kg/4 lb 8 oz mixed fish and seafood

 2 litres/3½ pints chicken stock

Spanish Paella

1. Shell the peas. Deseed and dice the red peppers and green peppers.

2. Heat the oil in a paella pan, add the diced peppers and the rice and cook over a medium heat, stirring. Add the wine and season to taste with salt and pepper. Sprinkle with saffron.

3. Add the fish and seafood to the rice.

4. Pour in the stock, add the peas and cook for about 20 minutes.

Serve directly from the paella pan.

This paella will serve 6–8 people.

■ Use Spanish short-grain rice for best results. Italian short-grain rice could make the dish very thick and rich. Other shellfish, chicken or rabbit meat can also be used.

250 g/9 oz chicken legs

 1 bunch fresh coriander

 100 g/3½ oz green peppers

 100 g/3½ oz red peppers

 80 g/2¾ oz leeks

 4 garlic cloves

 400 g/14 oz long-grain rice

 5 tbsp vegetable oil

 1 tbsp sugar

 4 tbsp soy sauce

 2 tbsp brown rice vinegar

 100 g/3½ oz prawns

 2 eggs

Fried Rice

1. Using a knife, remove the bones from the chicken and cut the meat into strips. Roughly chop the coriander, reserving a few sprigs to garnish. Deseed the green peppers and red peppers and cut them into quarters then into strips. Cut the leek in thin strips lengthways. Peel and thinly slice the garlic. Cook the rice according to the packet instructions. Heat the oil in a wok, add the chicken strips and cook, stirring, until brown. Using a slotted spoon, remove the chicken from the wok.

2. Add the garlic to the wok, sauté until golden, then add the green peppers and red peppers, mix well and cook for 2–3 minutes.

3. Add the leeks and chicken to the wok, then add the sugar, soy sauce and a little vinegar and mix well. Cook for 1 minute, stirring constantly.

4. Add the rice and prawns and cook for a further 3 minutes.

5. Beat the eggs in a bowl with a fork. Push the rice to one side. Add the eggs to the centre of the wok and cook, carefully stirring as they solidify.

6. Mix the rice with the eggs, then add the coriander and mix well. Drizzle the remaining vinegar over the rice.

Serve immediately in shallow bowls, garnished with the reserved coriander.

 45

■ Basmati rice can be used instead of long-grain rice. Other good vegetables for this dish are beansprouts, small broccoli florets, mangetout, baby corn and pak choi.

1 pork shoulder, weighing
1 kg/2 lb 4 oz

 1 tsp salt
pinch of black pepper

 2 tbsp sweet paprika

 1 tsp dried marjoram

 1 tbsp plain flour, for dusting

 300 g/10½ oz onions

 3 garlic cloves

 20 g/¾ oz fresh parsley sprigs

 40 g/1½ oz pork lard

 1 strip lemon zest

 ½ tsp caraway seeds

 4 tsp butter, softened, plus extra
to serve

 1 tbsp tomato purée

 500 ml/18 fl oz chicken stock or
beef stock

 500 g/1 lb 2 oz cooked
ribbon pasta, to serve

 snipped fresh chives, to garnish

Pork Goulash with Paprika & Butter Noodles

1. Cut the pork shoulder into 4-cm/1½-inch cubes. Leave the sinew and the fat on the meat, as they will make the goulash tender and juicy. Put the meat into a bowl, season with the salt, pepper, paprika and marjoram and dust with the flour.

2. Mix together well using your hands. Cut the onions into strips. Peel and finely dice 2 of the garlic cloves. Tie the parsley sprigs together with string.

3. Heat the lard in a large saucepan, then add the diced garlic, followed by the onions. Gently sauté until the onions are translucent. Finely chop the remaining garlic clove, the lemon zest and the caraway seeds, then combine them with the butter. Chill the herb butter in the refrigerator.

4. Put the meat in the pan and gently sauté for 10 minutes, being careful not to brown it. Push the meat to the side, add the tomato purée to the centre of the pan and lightly brown. Mix it with the meat, cover the pan and cook for a further 10 minutes.

*
* 120
*

■ For a Szegedin goulash, add 500 g/1 lb 2 oz of cooked sauerkraut and mix 150 g/5½ oz of crème fraîche into the goulash. Serve with freshly cooked parsley potatoes and bread dumplings.

5. Pour in the stock, re-cover the pan and cook over a low heat for 1 hour. Stir occasionally, adding water, if necessary. After 45 minutes' cooking, add the parsley and cook for a further 15 minutes. Remove the parsley, add the chilled herb butter and mix well.

Arrange the goulash on plates. Serve with pasta tossed in butter and sprinkled with chives.

1 leg of lamb, about 1.3 kg/3 lb

 bunch fresh parsley

 1 fresh tarragon sprig

 5 shallots

 150 g/5½ oz carrots

 3 onions

 1 head young cabbage

 2 garlic cloves

 300 g/10½ oz potatoes

 2 tbsp vegetable oil

 salt and pepper

 ½ tsp tomato purée

 1 bay leaf

 1.2 litres/2 pints beef stock

①

Irish Stew with Young Cabbage & Carrots

1. Cut into the leg of lamb along the bone and remove it carefully from the meat with the tip of your knife. Remove the fat and gristle from the skin. Cut the meat into 3-cm/1¼-inch pieces. Pluck the leaves from the parsley and tarragon sprigs and set aside. They will be chopped shortly before they are added to the dish, in order to preserve their flavour and their essential oils.

2. Cut the shallots in half. Cut the carrots diagonally into 1-cm/½-inch thick slices. Halve the onions and cut them into strips. Remove the outer leaves from the cabbage, cut it in half, remove the stalk and cut it into 3-cm/1¼-inch cubes. Peel the garlic and finely chop. Peel the potatoes and cut into 3-cm/1¼-inch cubes.

3. Heat the oil in a saucepan, add the garlic and then the onion strips and cook until they are translucent. Season the meat with salt and pepper, add to the pan and gently sauté for 10 minutes. Push the meat to the side, add the tomato purée to the centre of the pan to brown it a little, then mix it with the meat. Add the bay leaf.

4. Pour the stock over the meat. You can use water as a substitute, but you will need to season the meat more if you do. Bring the stew to the boil, then simmer, covered, for 15 minutes.

120

■ Lamb shoulder can be used instead of leg of lamb, but it will have to be cooked for 15 minutes longer, as it is more marbled. The quantity of vegetables can be increased or other vegetables used according to your preference. French beans, celery and Savoy cabbage are every bit as delicious in this stew.

5. Add the carrots, shallots and potatoes and simmer, covered, for a further 10 minutes. Add the cabbage, mix all of the ingredients together and simmer for a further 20 minutes, then remove the bay leaf.

Finely chop the parsley and the tarragon, stir them into the pan, then serve the stew in soup bowls.

500 g/1 lb 2 oz pork mince

 2 tbsp oyster sauce

 400 ml//14 fl oz canned coconut milk

 1 tsp red curry paste

 300 g/10½ oz canned sweetcorn, drained

 2 tbsp flaked almonds

Pork Meatballs Cooked in a Coconut-curry Sauce

1. Preheat the oven to 180°C/350°F/ Gas Mark 4. Mix the pork with the oyster sauce and shape into small balls. Put them into a shallow ovenproof dish. Pour the coconut milk into a tall container.

2. Add the curry paste to the coconut milk and stir.

3. Using a hand-held blender, blend the mixture briefly, until the curry paste is thoroughly mixed in.

4. Pour the sauce over the meatballs. Sprinkle over the sweetcorn, followed by the flaked almonds. Cook in the preheated oven for about 25 minutes, covered with foil to prevent the flaked almonds burning.

Transfer the meatballs to bowls and serve immediately.

■ Milder yellow curry paste can be used instead of the red curry paste. A few petits pois can be added to the sauce as well.

10 spicy lamb sausages

 2 tbsp vegetable oil

 1 garlic clove, peeled and sliced

 2 onions, finely sliced

 2 fresh rosemary sprigs

 2 bay leaves

 300 g/10½ oz white kidney beans, soaked overnight

 1 tsp tomato purée

 400 g/14 oz canned peeled tomatoes

 salt and pepper

Tomato Bean Stew with Spicy Lamb Sausage

1. Put the sausages into a saucepan with the oil and cook until brown all over. Add the garlic and cook until toasted.

2. Remove the sausages from the pan and set aside. Add the onions to the pan with the rosemary and bay leaves and cook until the onions are translucent. Push them to the side of the pan.

3. Drain the beans and add to the pan.

4. Add the tomato purée and the tomatoes to the pan, breaking down the tomatoes with a wooden spoon. Add salt and pepper to taste.

5. Pour cold water over the beans until they are covered. Return the sausages to the pan, bring to the boil, boil for 10 minutes, then cover, reduce the heat and simmer gently for 1 hour. Stir frequently, adding water as necessary to keep the beans just covered so they can cook completely.

Serve the bean stew in bowls with the lamb sausages on top.

+ 12 hours' soaking

■ Stew 2 fried duck legs, 1 piece of bacon and a few pieces of lamb with the beans and you have a wonderful cassoulet!

1 kg/2 lb 4 oz lamb shoulder

 salt and pepper

 5 garlic cloves

 350 g/12 oz onions

 3½ tbsp vegetable oil

 2 cinnamon sticks

 6 star anise

 ½ tsp curry powder

 1 tsp ground cumin

 2 tbsp tomato purée

 600 g/1 lb 5 oz canned peeled tomatoes

 250 g/9 oz basmati rice, steamed

 12 saffron threads

Biryani Rice with Lamb

1. Cut the lamb into 3-cm/1¼-inch cubes, then add salt and pepper to taste. Peel and thinly slice the garlic. Thinly slice the onion. Heat the oil in a wide saucepan. Add the garlic, cinnamon, star anise and onions and cook for 5 minutes until the onions are translucent. Season to taste with salt.

2. Add the lamb and cook, stirring, until brown, then sprinkle the lamb with the curry powder and cumin. Continue to cook for a further 10 minutes, making sure the spices don't toast too long as they can get bitter.

3. Push the meat to the side of the pan, add the tomato purée to the centre and sauté. Add the tomatoes with their can juices and bring to the boil, then cover and cook over a medium heat for about 40 minutes.

4. Use a fork to test whether the lamb is done. Remove the cinnamon sticks and the star anise and reserve to garnish.

5. Soak the saffron threads in 3½ tbsp water, then heat until the liquid is reduced to half its volume. Spread the rice over the lamb, drizzle over the water-soaked saffron, cover and heat for 5 minutes.

Garnish with the reserved cinnamon sticks and star anise and serve immediately in shallow bowls.

■ Sprinkle with chopped fresh mint and serve with natural yogurt. Indian restaurants sometimes lay a few pieces of gold leaf on top of this dish.

※
※ **100**
※

2 heads romanesco

 3 shallots

 2 tomatoes

 1 bunch fresh coriander

 2.5-cm/1-inch piece fresh ginger

 400 g/14 oz beef fillet steak

 4 tbsp oyster sauce

 4 tbsp groundnut oil

 1 garlic clove

 pinch of sugar

 juice of 1 lime

Vietnamese Beef Stew with Ginger

1. Wash the romanesco and divide it into florets, including the stalk. Slice the shallots lengthways. Cut the tomatoes into quarters, deseed and cut each quarter twice. Chop the coriander. Peel the ginger and finely slice. Remove any fat or tendons from the beef and cut the meat into strips 2-cm/¾-inch wide and 3-cm/1¼-inch long. Place the beef in a bowl, combine with the oyster sauce and marinate for 20 minutes.

2. Heat half of the oil in a non-stick wok, add the romanesco and sauté for about 3 minutes. Move the florets to the side, then pour the remaining oil into the opposite side of the wok.

3. Chop the garlic, add to the wok and sauté. Add the beef strips and sear for 1 minute, stirring constantly.

4. Add the shallots, ginger and tomato pieces and toss. Fry only briefly, so the vegetables remain crisp.

5. Add the coriander, sugar and lime juice. Mix once.

Transfer to bowls and serve immediately.

■ You can mix cooked glass noodles or wide rice noodles into this dish. You will need about 200 g/7 oz cooked noodles.

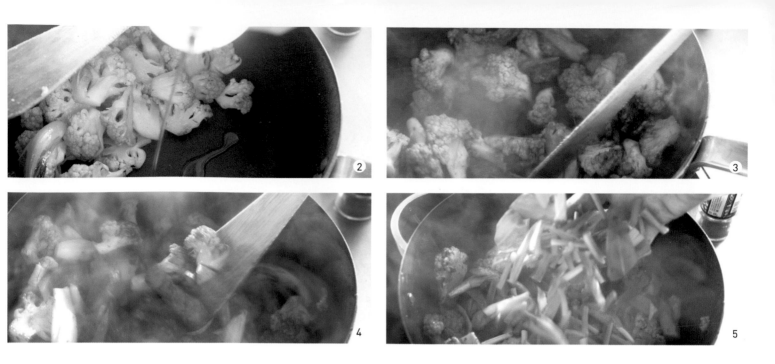

2 saddles of lamb, 1–1.2 kg/
2 lb 4 oz–2 lb 8 oz each

 salt and pepper

 3 tbsp olive oil

 6 garlic cloves

 2 fresh rosemary sprigs

 30 g/1 oz butter

Pink Roast Rack of Lamb with Rosemary

1. Put the saddles of lamb on a chopping board and cut into the skin under the loin fillet at a depth of 1 cm/½ inch.

2. Trim the skin and the meat from the ribs.

3. Shave the skin off the bone with the knife, so that it is easier to remove.

4. Carefully loosen the skin from the bone with your fingers until the bone is exposed and clean.

5. Turn it over and cut this part of the skin off.

6. Cut along the backbone and remove the white sinew carefully. Then continue cutting on the back to the ribs.

7. Turn over again and separate the rack of lamb from the backbone with sharp kitchen shears.

8. Remove the small bits of sinew and bones from the separated rack of lamb and season it with salt and pepper on both sides.

*
** **60**
*

■ You can use ready-prepared racks of lamb instead of saddle of lamb but you will still need to clean the ribs. The rack of lamb can also be roasted with a pecan-lemon marinade. Roughly chop some pecan nuts, cut 2 pieces of lemon zest into fine strips and mix them with 1 fresh rosemary sprig, 2 tablespoons of olive oil and 1 teaspoon of wholegrain mustard. Roast the lamb with this mixture for the last 5 minutes of cooking. Potatoes au gratin and French beans are very good accompaniments for rack of lamb.

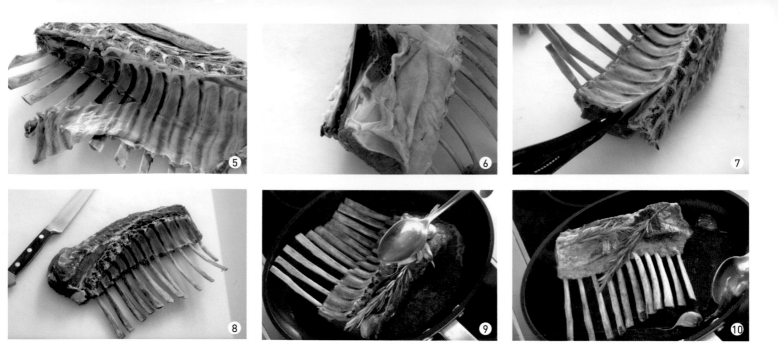

9. Preheat the oven to 180°C/350°F/Gas Mark 4. Heat the oil in a wide, ovenproof frying pan and put the rack of lamb in it top side down. Place the unpeeled garlic cloves in a bowl and press down on them with the heel of your hand. Add the garlic and the rosemary to the rack. Baste the lamb with the pan juices and turn it over after 5 minutes, replacing the rosemary on top of the rack so that it doesn't burn in the pan.

10. Add the butter and roast in the preheated oven for about 10 minutes, basting frequently.

Remove from the oven, cover with foil and leave to rest for 3 minutes before serving.

150 g/5½ oz onions

 400 g/14 oz beef rump steak

 4 tbsp vegetable oil

 1 dried red pepper

 salt and pepper

 3 tbsp sweet paprika

 1 tbsp tomato purée

 300 g/10½ oz long-grain rice

 150 g/5½ oz canned sweetcorn

Hungarian Paprikash with Corn

1. Thinly slice the onion. Slice the beef, then cut it into strips. Heat the oil in a large saucepan over a medium heat, add the onions and cook until translucent. Add the dried pepper.

2. Add the beef, and salt and pepper to taste, sprinkle with paprika and gently sauté. Push the beef to one side, add the tomato purée to the centre of the pan and lightly sauté, to reduce the acidity.

3. Add the rice, mix well and cook.

4. Drain the sweetcorn and add to the rice. Add plenty of water, bring to the boil, cover and cook for about 25 minutes over a medium heat. Stir occasionally, adding more liquid as necessary.

5. The dish is cooked when the rice has completely absorbed the liquid.

Transfer to plates and serve, sprinkled with paprika.

■ Beef stock can be used as a substitute for water, giving the dish more flavour. Red and yellow peppers, cut into strips, can also be added.

5 juniper berries

 5 white peppercorns

 2 onions

 160 g/5¾ oz carrots

 160 g/5¾ oz leeks

 160 g/5¾ oz celery

 1 tbsp coarse sea salt

 1 kg/2 lb 4 oz stewing beef

 2 cloves

 1 bay leaf

 fresh flat-leaf parsley, to garnish

snipped fresh chives, to garnish

1

Beef Stew with Root Vegetables & Herbs

1. Using the flat side of a knife, lightly crush the juniper berries and peppercorns.

2. Halve the unpeeled onions and cut off the root ends. Halve the carrots and cut the leeks and celery into 2 or 3 pieces, depending on their size.

3. Bring a large saucepan of lightly salted water to the boil, add the beef and simmer for about 1 hour.

4. Add the onions, carrots, leeks, celery, juniper berries, peppercorns, cloves and bay leaf and simmer for a further hour.

5. Season to taste with salt and pepper.

Cut the vegetables into bite-sized pieces and arrange them on a serving platter with the beef. Sprinkle with parsley and chives and serve.

* * * 120

■ Serve with parsley potatoes, fried potatoes or creamed spinach. This dish tastes delicious with tartare sauce.

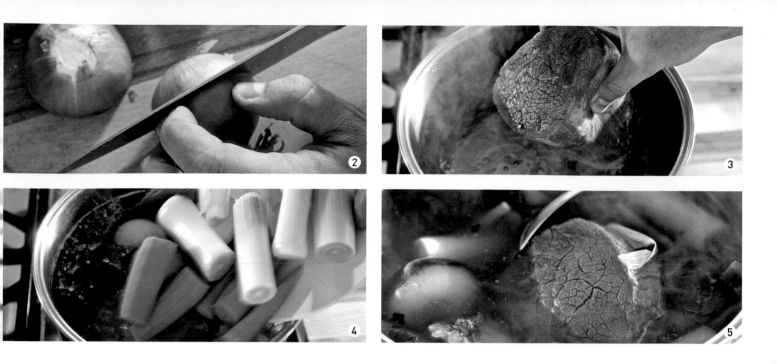

100 g/3½ oz butter, softened

 1 egg, plus 1 egg yolk

 1 tsp chopped fresh parsley

 pinch of salt

 pinch of freshly grated nutmeg

 60 g/2¼ oz self-raising flour

 plain flour, for dusting

 2 litres/3½ pints chicken stock

Chicken Soup with Butter Dumplings & Nutmeg

1. Whip the butter until holding peaks. Add the egg, egg yolk, parsley, salt, and nutmeg to taste. Beat until blended.

2. Using a rubber spatula, work in the self-raising flour and set aside for 10 minutes.

3. Use two teaspoons to shape the mixture into dumplings.

4. Put the dumplings on a board dusted with flour and chill in the refrigerator for 30 minutes.

5. Put the stock into a large saucepan, bring to the boil and add the dumplings. Simmer until the dumplings float, then cover and leave to stand for 25 minutes.

Serve in soup bowls, sprinkled with nutmeg to taste.

90

■ Julienned root vegetables boiled in salted water and some chicken meat can be added to this dish.

300 g/10½ oz egg noodles

 5 tbsp vegetable oil

 6 dried red chillies

 2 carrots

 200 g/7 oz broccoli

 2 skinless chicken breasts

 2 tbsp black bean paste

 100 g/3½ oz beansprouts

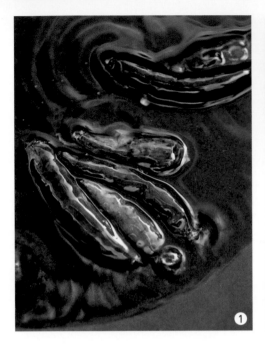

Shanghai-style Fried Egg Noodles with Chicken

1. Cook the egg noodles according to the packet instructions. Heat the oil in a wok, add the chillies and lightly brown.

2. Halve the carrots and slice diagonally. Cut the broccoli into florets. Add the carrots and broccoli to the wok and fry for 3 minutes, turning frequently.

3. Cut the chicken breasts into thin strips and add to the wok. Add the black bean paste, mix and continue stirring.

4. Add the noodles and beansprouts, stir and continue frying.

Transfer to plates and serve immediately.

■ Other vegetables that go well with this dish are green asparagus, peppers and pak choi.

 4 duck breasts, 200 g/7 oz each

 2 oranges

 salt and pepper

 1 tbsp vegetable oil

 100 ml/3½ fl oz Cointreau

 200 ml/7 fl oz orange juice

 2 tbsp pickled green peppercorns

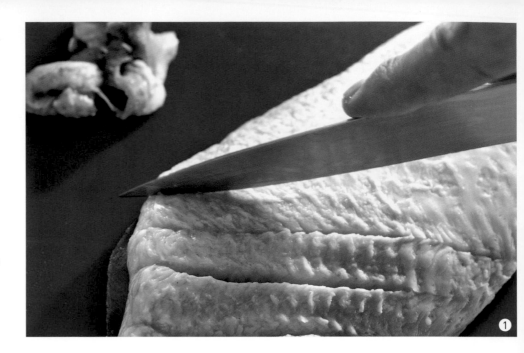

Roast Duck Breast with Orange-pepper Sauce

1. Place the duck breasts on a chopping board, skin side up. Cut off the protruding skin. Using a sharp knife, cut the skin in a criss-cross pattern.

2. Grate the orange peel using a fine grater. Use a knife to cut off all the pith from the orange, then slice the orange.

3. Season the duck breast on both sides with salt and pepper. Heat the oil in a frying pan and place the breasts in the pan skin side down.

4. Fry the breasts over a medium heat for about 10 minutes on each side, basting frequently with the duck fat. Continue to cook on the skin side until the skin is very crisp.

5. Arrange the duck breasts skin side up on a serving platter and leave to stand. Remove the fat from the pan, place the orange peel in the pan and add the Cointreau to the jus. Add the orange juice, peppercorns and orange slices.

Serve the duck breasts on warmed plates with the orange-pepper sauce.

■ Score the skin quite deeply to ensure that the fat escapes, otherwise the skin won't be very crisp.

1 whole duck

 3 shallots

 1 small apple

 salt and pepper

 1 garlic clove

 ½ bunch fresh marjoram

 250 ml/9 fl oz water

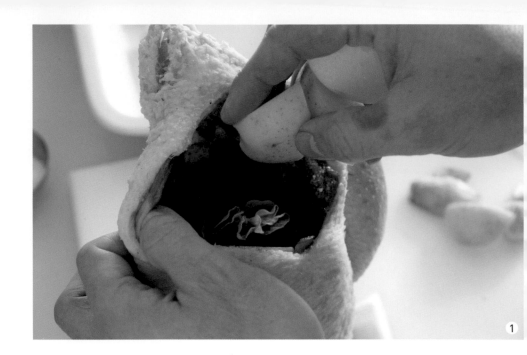

Roast Duck with Apples

1. Ask your butcher to prepare the duck so it is ready to cook and to pack the neck, wings and giblets separately. Preheat the oven to 180°C/350°F/ Gas Mark 4. Halve the shallots. Core the apple and cut into quarters, then slice the quarters in half. Clean the inside of the duck and rub dry with kitchen paper. Season to taste with salt and pepper. Stuff the duck with the unpeeled garlic clove, the shallots, the apple and a marjoram sprig.

2. Close the opening with cocktail sticks and tie with string. Cut off the ends of the cocktail sticks with scissors on both sides. This prevents the juices oozing out during cooking and keeps the flavour in the duck. Pluck any remaining pin feathers from the skin using small pliers.

3. Season the outside of the duck with salt and pepper and rub in well.

 **140**

■ Serve the duck with golden potato cakes, Brussels sprouts, red cabbage or sauerkraut. Strain the jus using a fine sieve and serve as a sauce. This jus is highly concentrated, so a little sprinkled carefully on the side of the plate is enough.

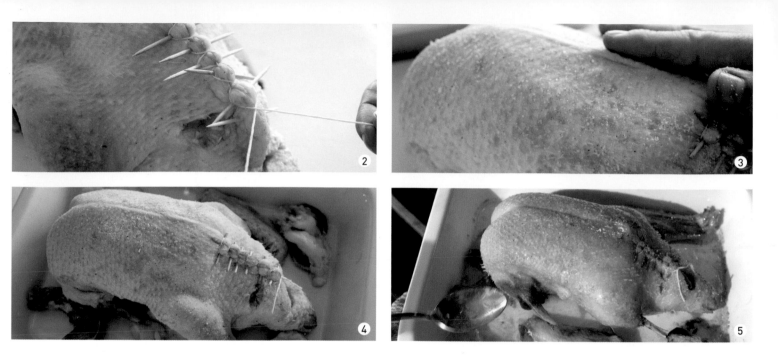

4. Place the duck and the giblets in a roasting dish. Pour in half the water and place on the lower shelf of the preheated oven.

5. Baste the duck with the cooking jus. After about 45 minutes, add the remaining water and roast the duck for a further 45 minutes. Loosen the string with a knife and remove the cocktail sticks.

Place the duck on a large serving platter, garnish with marjoram sprigs and serve.

500 g/1 lb 2 oz pinto beans

 80 g/2¾ oz carrots

 80 g/2¾ oz celery

 2 garlic cloves

 80 g/2¾ oz onions

 2 tbsp olive oil

 4 fresh rosemary sprigs

 3 bay leaves

 1 tsp fennel seeds, chopped

 1 tbsp tomato purée

 200 ml/7 fl oz white wine

 salt and pepper

 2 litres/3½ pints chicken stock

 2 duck breasts

Pinto Bean Ragout with Roast Duck Breast

1. Soak the beans for at least 2 hours. Cut the carrots and celery into 5-mm/ ¼-inch pieces. Crush the garlic cloves into a bowl, then dice the onions. Heat the oil in a shallow saucepan, then add the onions, carrots and celery to the pan and gently sweat for 10 minutes.

2. Add the rosemary, bay leaves, fennel seeds and garlic and lightly sauté.

3. Push the vegetables to one side of the pan. Add the tomato purée to the centre of the pan so it loses its acidity. Add the wine, allowing the liquid to reduce.

4. Drain the beans, add to the pan and sauté for 2 minutes. Add salt and pepper to taste, then pour in the chicken stock and simmer gently for 50 minutes. Stir occasionally to prevent the beans sticking to the base of the pan. Stir carefully to avoid crushing them. Add a little water if necessary.

Meanwhile, cook the duck breasts (see page 54). Divide the beans between four serving plates, then slice the duck breasts, arrange on top of the beans and serve immediately.

+ 2 hours soaking time

80

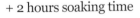

■ Fennel seeds are easier to chop if you drizzle them with a little oil beforehand to prevent them jumping. The pinto bean ragout also goes well with sausages or stuffed pigs' trotters.

4 pigeons

 4 slices of white bread

 1 shallot

 ½ bunch fresh parsley

 100 g/3½ oz butter, softened

 2 eggs

 salt and pepper

 pinch of freshly grated nutmeg

 8 smoked bacon rashers

 4 garlic cloves

 10 juniper berries

 2 tbsp vegetable oil

 4 fresh rosemary sprigs

1

Stuffed Pigeons Wrapped in Bacon

1. Ask your butcher to prepare the pigeons so they are ready to cook and to pack the heart and liver separately. To make the stuffing, finely cube the heart and liver. Remove the crusts from the white bread and cut the bread into 5-mm/¼-inch cubes. Finely chop the shallot and the parsley. Beat the butter in a bowl until it is fluffy. Separate the eggs and add the yolks to the butter, one at a time. Season to taste with salt and pepper. Add the nutmeg and mix with a wire whisk, then add the shallot and parsley.

2. Add the liver, heart and bread cubes and mix carefully.

3. Rub the inside of the pigeons with kitchen paper and remove any skin and blood residues. Season inside and out with salt and pepper and fill with the stuffing.

4. Wrap each of the pigeons with 2 bacon rashers and tie together with string. Using the flat side of a knife, crush the unpeeled garlic and the juniper berries.

5. Preheat the oven to 220°C/425°F/ Gas Mark 7. Heat the oil in an ovenproof frying pan and place the pigeons, rosemary, juniper berries and garlic in the pan. Cook on one side until brown, then turn and brown on the other side. Transfer to the preheated oven and cook for about 25 minutes, frequently basting with the jus. Remove from the oven, take off the string and halve the pigeons lengthways using a sharp knife.

Arrange on plates and serve immediately.

■ Place any excess stuffing in a buttered soufflé dish and bake in the oven for about 15 minutes at 200°C/400°F/Gas Mark 6. The butter makes it easier to turn out the stuffing later. Pumpkin gratin and salsify, which is also called vegetable oyster, make wonderful accompaniments for the pigeon dinner.

✳
✳
✳

90

1 garlic bulb

 1 lemon

 bunch fresh parsley

 4 Cornish hens, each about 350 g/12 oz

 salt and pepper

 300 g/10½ oz small onions

 60 g/2¼ oz butter

Cornish Hens Roasted with Lemon & Garlic

1. Preheat the oven to 180°C/350°F/ Gas Mark 4. Set the garlic, stem upright, on a work surface and press down with the palm of your hand to loosen the cloves. Remove the outer skin and crush the cloves in their skins. Rinse the lemon under hot water and cut into 5-mm/¼-inch slices. Pluck the parsley off the stems. Wash the Cornish hens and dry them inside with kitchen paper.

2. Thoroughly season the hens, inside and out, with salt and pepper. Stuff with the pressed garlic cloves and the parsley, reserving some of the parsley to garnish.

3. Place the stuffed hens in a roasting tin. Cut off the stalk end of the onions but do not peel. Arrange the onions and lemon slices around the hens. Distribute the butter over the hens.

4. Roast for 25 minutes in the preheated oven. Add 100 ml/3½ fl oz water to the tin and scrape the base with a wooden spoon to loosen the sediment. Baste the hens with the jus and roast for a further 15 minutes. Remove from the oven.

Serve the hens with the onions and jus, garnished with the remaining parsley.

✳✳✳ **80**

■ Be careful not to injure the skin when you pluck the remaining pinfeathers with fishbone pliers. The white meat would dry out at these spots. Cornish hens taste just as delicious cold. Serve with any type of potato dish.

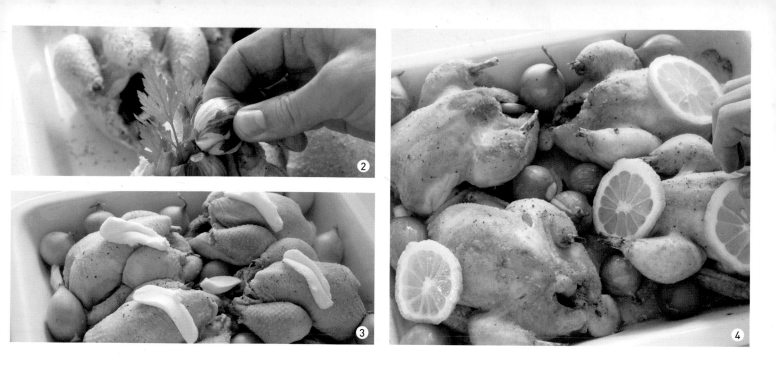

INDEX